COMMISSION: IMPOSSIBLE ROGUE AGENT

Eric Simon
Eric Lee

BR◯KE
AGENT

IngramSpark

The Broke Agent LLC

thebrokeagent@gmail.com

Publisher's Note: This is a work of fiction. Names, characters, places, and incidents are a product of the author's imagination. Locales and public names are sometimes used for atmospheric purposes. Any resemblance of actual people, living or dead, or to business, companies, events, institutions, or locales is completely coincidental.

PRINTED IN THE UNITED STATES OF AMERICA

Book design by Eric Lee

Graphics by Eric Lee

Illustrations by Eric Lee

Cover design by Eric Lee

First Edition

ISBN 978-0-578-42801-7

Real Estate / Sales

Humor / Comic Strips & Cartoons

This book is dedicated to everyone in the real estate industry who has supported The Broke Agent and laughed with me throughout the years. I know you cannot say what is on your mind because it might ruin your image and career. So, I will say it.

Check out The BA on all social platforms @TheBrokeAgent:

Blog: thebrokeagent.com
Store: thebrokeagentstore.com

Also, check out @realestate_squarepants on instagram for real estate related comics.

CONTENTS

4

13

20

21

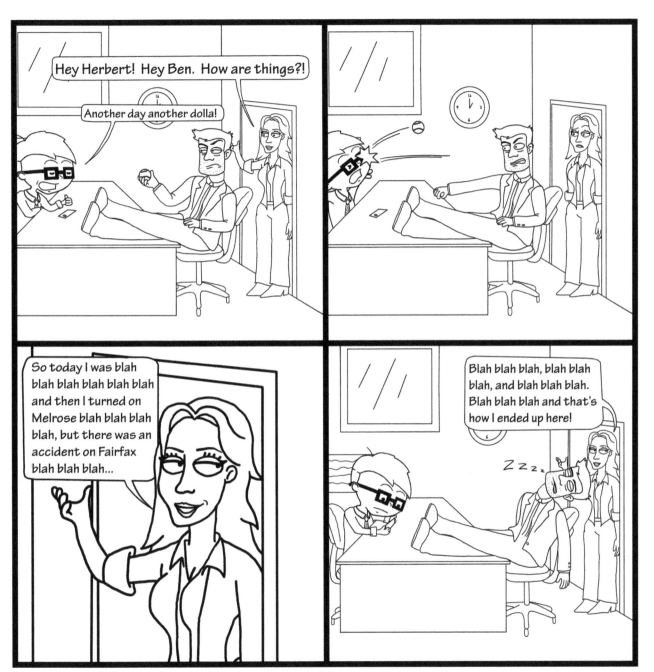

27

31

34

37

40

41

46

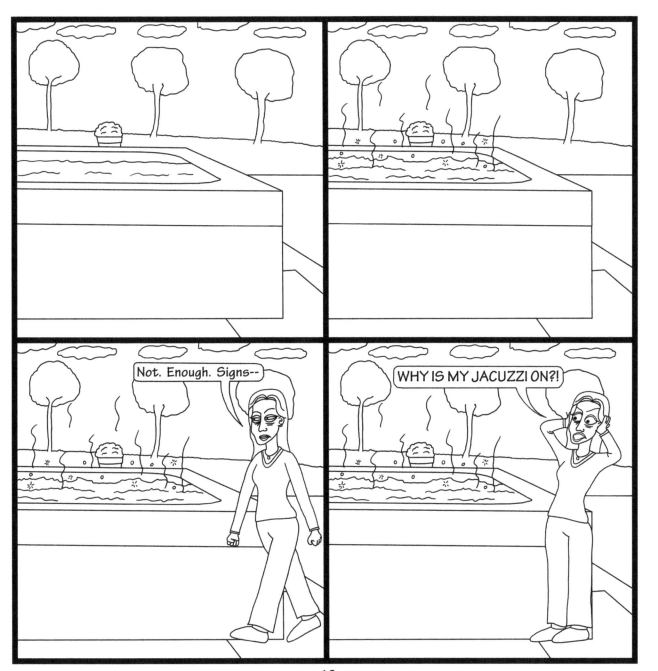

58

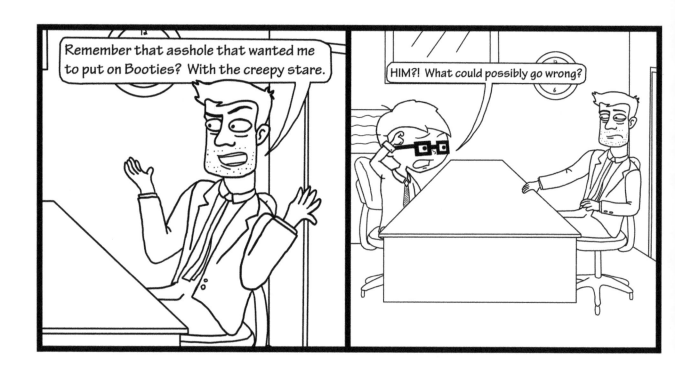

64

69

73

78

86

105

110

112

118

120

123

126

127

131

137

141

144

145

148

150

151

153

154

155

157

159

162

167

171

173

174

177

178

To be continued...

Author: Eric Simon aka The Broke Agent

I am the co-founder and CEO of The Broke Agent. I embody The
"BA" because I live it. Sitting dead open houses twice a week made
me crave a comedic outlet. I needed to unleash the thoughts and
inner monologue that came with the insane experiences I was
having as a young agent in Los Angeles. So, I combined my two
passions: sports and comedy... I mean real estate and
comedy... and created The Broke Agent with a friend. Traditional
real estate publications bored the hell out of me and everything I
read felt inauthentic and stale. I was tired of all the success
stories and wanted to read something more relatable. My goal is
to make this brand a staple in the real estate community and
provide some comedic relief to real estate professionals around
the world. Also, I want to get verified on Instagram
(@thebrokeagent). This book might help with that...

Illustrator and Co-Author: Eric Lee

As a real estate agent from Calgary, I "love" showing homes in
eight feet of snow and ice skating to my listing appointments. I
found my outlet by going back to my childhood hobby, doodling. So
now I draw real estate related comics on Instagram. If I can make
even one person smile (including myself), then I'm happy.

Check out The BA on all social platforms @TheBrokeAgent:

Blog: thebrokeagent.com
Store: thebrokeagentstore.com

Also, check out @realestate_squarepants on instagram for real estate related comics.